SoulCry : book one

HOPE
FOR THE WOUNDED SOUL

an intimate poetic
expression of the deep
longings and cries of the soul

The Lord listens to the suffering of
the afflicted ones crying for help.
Psalm 22:24 (paraphrased)

Trudy Colflesh

Bridal Cry

Bridalcry Publishing

Colorado Springs, CO

Copyright © 2010, revised 2018 by Trudy Colflesh

Cover and page design by Nathan Fisher, www.nathanfisher.com

ISBN 978-0-9848599-0-0

Additional Copies Available At

www.encouraginghope.com/books
www.amazon.com/author/trudycolflesh

Table of Contents

Foreword

As the reader of Hope for the Wounded Soul, you are about to embark on a journey to your heart. This book speaks the personal, often hidden thoughts we didn't know we had or couldn't express.

Have you wondered why you have trouble with relationships? Do you feel confident in who you are? Have you shut your emotional self down? Do you try to figure everything out logically? Are you angry a lot or do you even know what you feel? Do you feel loved? Are you afraid to let others really know you? You may not relate to every situation, but the emotional impact can be familiar.

Read the material at your own pace. Let the words speak what your heart may want to say. Listen to your inner self and believe what you are hearing. Show kindness and understanding to yourself as you discover what you need to know. Spend time writing and reflecting.

Allow your heavenly Father and Jesus the Son to comfort you and bring you to an understanding of truth and acceptance of yourself.

The truth in this book will bring you healing and freedom. You will step into the joy of knowing you are loved and will learn to walk in healing hope.

ABOUT THE NOTEBOOK PAGES:

The Soul is expressing its deep cries of emotion in the notebook pages.

About the Scroll:

The Lord responds to the cry of the Soul in the scrolls.

NICE

How do I know
If I stop being nice
You'll still want me?

I've worked so long,
I've worked so hard,
To be so good.

I do it longer,
I do it harder,
I do it best!

So you'll want me.

Don't you see how hard I try?
See how good I am?

I swallow my anger,
I ignore my hurt,
I forget my pain.

I smile...because I'm nice.
I'm really nice.

I'll earn your love
By how I act.
I'll deserve your love
By what I do.

I'm terrorized to think
Of not being nice.
My stomach knots and twists.

If you don't want me
I won't survive.
The risk is far too great.

Without your love
I'll die!

So I will be nice,
Really, really, nice,
And keep you wanting me.

AUTHOR'S COMMENTS

Many of us grew up in the time of society when we were expected to be polite and courteous to one another. The unspoken rule was, "If I am nice to you and take care of your wants, you will be nice to me and take care of mine."

The trouble with thinking like that was you had no control over your emotional needs. You depended upon others to meet them. Many times others didn't know the rules, or didn't want to take care of you, and you were left trying harder to "make" someone else treat you like they were "supposed to."

If you are operating emotionally from a younger self, it could feel like abandonment, or even death, if you weren't wanted or loved.

THOUGHTS TO JOURNAL

• Have I felt this way?

• If I were honest, what would I say about how I felt?

• What do I think would happen if I spoke honestly?

PRAYER

Dear Lord,
Help me to be honest with what I am feeling. I need to stop
pretending. I want people to know how I really feel and who I really
am. Teach me how to express myself lovingly, but firmly. Give me a
heart that chooses to show thoughtfulness and care, not out of fear,
but choice and love.

IMPRISONED IN GOODNESS

Frightened little child,
Huddled in the corner
Of your strong defense.

Long ago you figured out:
"If I make them happy
If I keep them happy
I'll be safe!"

So you were good,
And thoughtful,
And kind,
And caring,

And worked hard,
So very hard,
To be all that they needed.

Every good deed done for approval
Became another bar
Of protection
In your fortress of safety.

Reaching under the steel
Of your own defense
You furtively grabbed
Any crumbs of kindness
That fell your way.

Frightened and starving
You tried harder,
And harder,

To make them happy,
To keep them happy,
To try to stay needed,
To keep yourself safe.

But it all began to fail.

The defense of safety
Became bars of bondage
And you found yourself imprisoned
In goodness.

WAITING FOR TIME

Oh little child, so mute
So wordless
Waiting in the shadows
For someone to notice
How sad you look,
How sad you feel,
Waiting for someone to ask
And give you permission to say you feel
Sad,
And lonely.

You need time. Lots of time,
Extra time.
Special time.
Unhurried time.

Don't be ashamed,
It's not "silly" to feel.
Even if no one has time for you,
You can still be sad you don't receive it.

It's OK to be needy,
It's OK to be sad,
It's OK to take time

You need time. Lots of time.
Extra time.
Special time.
Unhurried time.
Relaxed time.

Not everyone is busy
I can give you time.
Let me hold you in my arms.
You are precious, you are mine.

SADNESS

Sadness.
Heaviness.
Sorrow.

So quiet, so undemanding, so good.

Yet so sad,
So hurt,
So alone.

She's alone inside.
No words to build exits.
Encased, inside with no words.
Only heavy, dark, and sad.

My older self
Felt the pain
And reached out to help.

I will teach you words
For heavy, dark, and sad,
Use them to build exits
To express.
And I will be there to hear
Your heavy, dark, and sad.

I hurt that you are hurt.
My tears fall as yours.
Let them float me into you
So you are not alone.

We will light a light.
We will build a bridge,
With feelings that have words
That bring us out to live.

Once you were lost
But now you are found.
Once you were no ones
But now you are the Lord's and mine.

AUTHOR'S COMMENTS

When you look deep inside your heart, do you find a part of you that is sad? How old do you feel? Have you ever thought to take some time and dialogue with those feelings?

Sometimes a person feels ashamed to admit they are needy. If your needs weren't met in a healthy way when you were younger, you may have decided you didn't have needs. It was less painful that way, and maybe safer.

But the need stayed, even if you denied you had needs. All of us have needs and are needy. Obvious needs are air, food, and sleep. Emotional needs that keep us healthy are love, attention, value, being wanted, time, laughter, and recreation, among others.

You can be your own best friend. You know yourself better than anyone else. Can you listen to your inner pain and show empathy? Can you encourage your inner self, like you would a friend?

THOUGHTS TO JOURNAL

• Do I feel ashamed to have needs?

• Do I know why?

• Give words to your feelings. This will help you validate yourself.

• What are my needs right now?

• How will I get them met in healthy ways?

PRAYER

Dear Lord,

I bring you all my unmet needs and wounded feelings. Help me to pay attention to myself and show love to the parts of me that feel abandoned. Thank you that you love me. Help me to love me too.

TO MY INNER CHILD

There is a place
Inside of me
For you to live and grow.

I want you here,
I need you here,
There's much for us to know.

This place is safe,
This place is free,
There is no price to pay.

I will not judge,
I will not shame,
I will not go away.

There is no obligation asked
For you to have me stay.
It is my heart,
It is my choice,
You need not be afraid.

I am your own,
And you are mine,
I'll always hold you dear.

Please come and dwell
In safety now,
I always want you here.

PERFECT CHILDHOOD

I had a perfect childhood,
You know.

Well, maybe not perfect
But it was really good.

I mean,
By comparison to others
It was fine.

The things that happened
Weren't all that bad,

They did the best they could.

Really, it's OK,
You don't need to feel sorry.

Oh, please, you're embarrassing me.
It wasn't that big a deal
What happened to me.

I'm not a cry baby.
Other kids had it worse.

My parents worked hard
to take care of me.

I'm not ungrateful.
I got through it, I survived.

It didn't hurt that much...
Or did it?

I'll be OK...
Or will I?

No, really, believe me.
It's got to be true.
My childhood was

Just...

...Fine.

FROZEN SHUT

Icicle bars piercing the heart
Growing with each
Cold command:

Stop laughing!
Stop shouting!
Stop crying!
Stop pouting!

A heart once filled with feeling
Slowly drains
And shivers.

It's not safe to feel.
There's no place to feel.
The heart constricts and hardens.

Icy thoughts grip your soul.
"What you feel is wrong."
"You don't really hurt."
"You don't really matter."

Your heart is encased.
You are growing numb.
Your feelings freeze in place.

You no longer feel how you feel.
All is covered over.
You are frozen shut!

THE THAW

You never intended a human heart
To be lifeless and dead,
Frozen shut from fear
Of failing.

You, O Lord, destined my heart
To be like yours.

You are alive and warm
And vibrant.
Your heart beats with
Compassion and goodness
And feels intensely.

You do not fear to feel.
For perfect love casts out fear.

Bring, O Lord, the light and warmth
Of your Presence
To shine upon my frozen heart.

Warm me with your love
That I may trust to tear
And know it's safe
To feel once more
Alive and free.

Laughing, shouting!
Crying, pouting!
Mad, sad, glad,
And scared!

Thaw each part, Lord.
Thaw it all,
Until my heart stirs and beats again
With feelings, with passion,
With intensity,
With LIFE!

AUTHOR'S COMMENTS

When a child is consistently abused in any way, they learn to shut themselves off from the painful emotions.

The problem with this attempt to not feel is that you lose touch with what's really going on with yourself emotionally. You move into your thinking and become a "walking head."

Do you have trouble feeling free with your emotions? Sometimes the only feeling you may be in touch with is anger or rage.

If anger is followed to its root, there is usually a quieter emotion like sadness or fear underneath the more protective aggressiveness. Allowing yourself to feel again is painful. There can be much to grieve.

Like lancing a boil, it hurts to open up to the infection, but it is the way healing begins.

As your backlog of grief is experienced, you begin to feel alive again.

THOUGHTS TO JOURNAL

- Have I minimized or discounted my childhood difficulties?

- Who has hurt me and how?

- What emotions am I numb to?

- Do I cry?

PRAYER

Dear Lord,

I forgive my parents for any failure on their part which has caused me pain in what I did or did not receive from them. Please break me out of my self-imposed prison of emotional numbness. Give me the courage to feel again and grieve the pain behind my numbness. I want to be fully alive. Breathe your life into my heart and let me feel.

FEEL THE PAIN

It's burning right beneath
The surface.

It's hot.
I'm afraid.
It's too painful
To feel the pain.

I'm not ready.
I'll put it off,
Settle down
Cover over.

Maybe later
I'll feel the pain.

Now's not a good time.
I've got to focus,
Force myself forward.
It will go away.

I can manage,
Keep busy
Deny, forget
The pain.

The tears that seep
I brush away.
The anger that rages
Drives people away.

But I'll manage.
I can't touch
What really hurts.

There's so much pain now
The real pain has to be worse...
Or is it?

TEARS

Tears seep
Tears weep
Tears flow.

Not ashamed,
You can see,
You can know.

It's not wrong
Or stupid, or dumb
To feel or cry.

Tears come with feelings.
They release the pain
And let me
And others know
I hurt.

I risk my tears
With you.
Please hold steady
And let me cry.

Don't take away
My need to feel
By insensitivity,
Impatience,
Or your own discomfort.

If you do,
The tears may stop
But the pain increases,
And I go inward,
Shut down, uncomforted,
And shamed.

But I will trust you with my tears,
And long to find comfort
In your just being here.

I FEEL ASHAMED

It's so hard
To look into your eyes.
I feel awkward, embarrassed,
Ashamed.

I manage a quick glance
To your face
Rapidly assessing
Your reaction to me.

If I see a smile,
Kind eyes holding steady
Toward me,
I smile inside
And long for more.

I want to drink deeply
Of your kind look,
But I would have to
Fix my eyes on yours.

It's just too risky,
Too frightening.
What might you see
Inside of me
If you had long enough
To look?

I can't bear having you know
I am flawed,
Defective, imperfect.
I desperately need your kindness and love,
Yet I can't risk receiving it.
I am so ashamed.

If your eyes locked with mine
You would see the real me
And surely turn away.

AUTHOR'S COMMENTS

Shame is one of the most painful of human emotions. Shame cuts to the core. Shame is a diminishing of your very self to a sense of disgrace. It's not just about what you have done, but rather an attack on who you are.

You may have grown up in a "shame filled" home. Attempts were made to control your behavior by attacking your personhood rather than correcting the problem.

You may have tried harder to please or you may have chosen to rebel. Either way, you still felt that inner shame of not measuring up.

THOUGHTS TO JOURNAL

• Do I keep a part of me hidden because of shame?

• What do I think would happen if I really opened up to someone?

• Do I believe there are some things I can't be forgiven for?

PRAYER

Dear Lord,

Help me to know that you are not ashamed of me. You know all about me, and you continue to love me. You love me because you want to love me. Please take this shame from me. Help me to see myself as you see me. Help me to love myself.

YOU MAKE ME SO MISERABLE!

You're the cause of all
My problems!
You make me so miserable!

Don't you know it's your job
To be aware of all my needs?

I can't believe you don't see how
Miserable you're making me!

I keep trying to tell you
How you're doing it all wrong!

All my time and energy
Goes into correcting
And directing you!

I know you so much better
than you know yourself.
I'm only doing this for your own good!
Why won't you listen?

I would be so much happier
If you were different!

I try so hard to
Change you,
But you're just so stubborn!

I'm so tired of being miserable!
Why won't you change?

Yet, you just ignore
All my good advice and pleas
And keep on being...
Yourself.

NOBODY MAKES YOU MISERABLE

Nobody makes you miserable,
My child!

Your sadness is from within,
Not without.

Use your energy
To love and heal yourself.
Don't wait for others
To notice.

I notice.
Now you notice.

You know best what you need.
Find ways to meet those needs
In healthy ways.

Others are not responsible
For your happiness.
You are!

You can't change others,
But you can change
Yourself.

There is hope for change
When you are in charge
Of you.

I have created you to be
Yourself.

Accept others for
Themselves.

Different from you is not wrong.
It's just different.

You can be happy and free.
Choose yourself,
And choose me.

I AM ANGRY!

I AM ANGRY!

IT WASN'T FAIR!
MY CHILDHOOD NEEDS WEREN'T MET!

COULDN'T THEY SEE?

WHY DIDN'T THEY CARE?

WHERE WERE THEY WHEN I NEEDED THEM -
TOO BUSY, TOO HURRIED, TOO EXHAUSTED
ASSUMING I WAS OK?

BUT THEY NEVER STOPPED TO NOTICE,
OR FIND OUT.

I TRIED TO BE GOOD, DO WHAT THEY
WANTED, NOT BE A BURDEN.

THEY WERE ALREADY DEALING WITH
ENOUGH, I DIDN'T WANT TO
GIVE THEM MORE.

SO I CAME UP WITH A SOLUTION:

SINCE NOBODY NOTICED MY NEEDS,
I DECIDED TO STOP FEELING THEM.

I DECIDED IT DIDN'T MATTER IF I HAD NEEDS,
CAUSE NOBODY CARED ANYWAY.

I WAS FINE JUST THE WAY I WAS.
I COULD TAKE CARE OF MYSELF.
I DIDN'T NEED ANYONE -
TO NOTICE, TO CARE.

"I DON'T CARE," "THAT DIDN'T HURT,"
"SO WHAT," "LEAVE ME ALONE,"
"I'LL DO IT MYSELF,"

"I DON'T NEED YOU,
WANT YOU, LIKE YOU,"
"I DON'T HURT, I DON'T FEEL,
I DON'T KNOW,"

"I DON'T CRY,"

more...

I'M STILL ANGRY,
EVEN THOUGH I'M GROWN!

NOW IT'S NOT ABOUT MY PARENTS
IT'S ABOUT YOU!

BUT YOU'LL NEVER KNOW
CAUSE I WON'T TELL YOU.
BESIDES, WHO CARES?

I DON'T EVEN CARE ANYMORE
IF YOU REACH OUT TO ME.

I'LL NEVER TELL YOU HOW I FEEL, HOW I HURT.

IF YOU REALLY CARED, YOU'D KNOW.
CERTAINLY YOU WOULD NOTICE
SOMETHING IS WRONG.

YOU WOULD SPEND TIME WITH ME,
WAIT PATIENTLY, NOT GIVE UP ON ME,

ASK ME, ENCOURAGE ME, DRAW ME OUT,
GIVE ME WORDS,
SEE PAST MY DEFENSE.

YOU WOULD HOLD ON THROUGH MY ANGER,

SEE THE WOUNDS,
HEAR THE SOBS,
COMFORT THE PAIN - SURELY YOU WOULD KNOW.

BUT THEY DIDN'T
AND NOW YOU DON'T!

AND I AM ANGRY!

AND I WILL PUNISH YOU FOR
WHAT THEY DIDN'T DO.

I WILL WITHDRAW.
I WILL PRETEND I'M FINE.

I WILL HATE YOU FOR NOT KNOWING.
I WILL JUDGE YOU FOR
NOT RESCUING ME.

more...

I WILL BE ANGRY AND MAKE
YOU GUESS WHAT'S WRONG,

BUT I WILL NOT TELL YOU WHEN YOU ASK
BECAUSE I DON'T BELIEVE YOU CARE.

I WILL SEE THAT YOU NEVER WIN
BECAUSE I DON'T TRUST YOU.

THEY DIDN'T COMFORT ME.
HOW COULD YOU?
HOW COULD I EVEN START TO LET YOU COME CLOSE?

I FEEL SUCH SCORCHING PAIN AND
EMBARRASSMENT
TO ADMIT THE TRUTH
THAT I NEED COMFORT,
TENDERNESS, AND TIME.

WILL I BE SHAMED ONCE AGAIN?

ITS FAR EASIER TO BE ANGRY.

ITS ONLY SAFE TO HAVE NEEDS IF SOMEBODY CARES THAT I HAVE THEM.

ARE YOU THAT SOMEBODY?

DO YOU CARE?

DO YOU REALLY, REALLY CARE?

I WANT YOU TO CARE.

I NEED YOU TO CARE.

HELP ME! PLEASE HELP ME!

PLEASE CARE.

AUTHORS COMMENTS

Urealistic expectations can be a huge underlying source of anger. Are you looking to someone or something besides yourself to meet certain needs in you? Are you expecting your spouse/best friend/boss to take care of an emotional need? Usually this need is unspoken. The other person cannot read your mind. They do not know they are "letting you down," or not meeting some other need of yours which you believe should be met.

First look inside yourself to determine what expectation you have of the other person. Is it realistic for them to meet the requirement that you believe they should meet? (See "You Make Me So Miserable," page 34)

If the expectation/desire seems reasonable to you, then you can verbalize that to the other person. The person then has the choice to meet or not meet your request. You cannot force another person to meet your needs without your control and manipulation.

The truth is, you are responsible to see how realistic your needs are, who's responsible to meet them, and how to get them met in a healthy way.

THOUGHTS TO JOURNAL

• Am I angry more times than happy?

• If I weren't angry, how would I feel?

• Finish the sentence, "I am angry because…"

• This will help you find other emotions, like disappointed, rejected, hurt.

PRAYER

Dear Lord,

I don't want to be an angry person. Please take this anger from me. Allow me to touch the other feelings I have beneath the anger, and share them with those I am hurting. Help me stop assuming I know what others are thinking. Help me to stop having knee-jerk reactions toward them. Grant me the ability to calm myself and find out what is really going on between me and others when I start to feel anger.

PROVE YOU LOVE ME

I need you to show me love.
I need you to tell me I'm special.

But it's never enough.
I need lots of reassurance you know,
Sometimes a bottomless pit.

I don't mean to suck you dry,
But I'm so needy.

Even when you tell me you love me
I don't believe it.

How can I know you really mean it?
Especially when I'm angry and hurtful.
Maybe you're just appeasing me,
Not really caring...

And that makes me mad.
I can't stand when you try so hard
Being sweet and forgiving.

You can't possibly mean it
When I'm so nasty to you.

But maybe I can have some relief
From the torment of my pain
By projecting it on to you.

If you really love me
You will prove it by enduring
My abuse.

I'll probably drive you away,
But even if you stay and stand
against the torrent
Of my anger to prove your love,

I still won't believe you.
I can never believe that you love me
Because I don't love myself.

I can never let you close enough
to know the truth —
That there's nothing in me
To love.

CONTAIN THE LOVE

Sad driven child
So hungry for love.

Crumbs fall from the table
Which you quickly devour.
But they never satisfy.

You pant at others' feet
For tokens of love
And bite the very hand
That gives.

People turn away
And you prove to yourself again
The lie
That there's nothing in you to love.

Come to my banqueting table, my child.
Sit with me, Father God invites.

You are loved for I made you lovable.
I give you value and worth because you are mine.

Let me build in you a leak proof container
For my love.
Let me fill it with acceptance, hope and joy.

Hold onto love by believing it's for you.
Receive my gift of love.
I gave my Son as proof and seal
Of my eternal desire for you.

Believe in me, believe in you.
Believe you're loved
Through and through.

Be saturated with my love.
There is more than enough.
You are always included
In my bountiful supply.

MAKING MYSELF THE LOSER

I've figured out
How to keep making myself the loser
No matter how much I try to win.

I set up a standard of
Impossible shoulds and oughts
And assign them Divine authority.

Then when I fail
My own self-imposed rules
I can feel unworthy and angry

And rail against God
For His unfairness
To me,

Followed by feeling guilty
For being angry at the One
Who loves me,

And miserable for not obeying
What I decided He wanted,
No matter how hard I try.

It's so unfair!
I'm so miserable!
I'm such a loser!

I just can't win!

AUTHOR'S COMMENTS

Human beings are designed to be loved and to give love. If you didn't receive loving nurture early in your life, you start to believe it is your fault that your need for love is not being met.

Often, the more you desperately want to be loved, the more you fight (out of lack of trust) anyone who tries to give it, thereby proving to yourself yet again that you are unlovable.

Other times, you may exhaust the people who show you kindness by requiring and expecting them, unknowingly to both of you, to make up for all your unmet needs. These ways of thinking will quickly destroy an adult relationship.

THOUGHTS TO JOURNAL

• Can I accept compliments?

• Do I believe someone really means it
when they say they love me?

• Why or why not?

• What parts of me do I think are
unacceptable to others? To God?

PRAYER

Dear Lord,

Give me the courage to tell you what I don't like about myself. Let me hear what you want to say to me. I offer to you the defenses I have built to keep love away from my heart. Help me admit to others that I need to hear words of kindness and care.

I DON'T WANT TO GROW UP

I don't want to grow up!
I don't want to be responsible
For me!

It's not fair!
I've been waiting all my life
For someone to take care of me,
To make life fun,
To keep me happy.

If I grow up
I let go of my dream
That someone out there
Will someday give me
What I never got.

I have waited so long
And tried so hard
To tell others how to do it right
So they could take care of me.
But they just won't learn!

So I keep looking,
And dreaming,
Investing a lifetime,
Waiting for that one

Who will care for all my needs,
Notice all my distresses,
Kiss away all my hurts.

I have great faith I will someday
Find him.
So I will wait
For my prince to arrive,

And stay little and small
To delight him
When he comes.

IF I GROW UP

If I grow up,
Take responsibility for myself,
I'm afraid
I won't do it right.

If I stay small
And weak
There won't be as much
Required of me.

I'll be able to fail,
Make mistakes,
And not judge myself,

Because I'm immature,
Unaware,
Unknowing.

Grown-ups must be perfect
You know.
I could never measure up.

No one would want me
If I didn't do it right.

If I was disapproved of,
I would die!

It's just too risky
To take that step
Into grown-up.

Others may judge me now for my
Irresponsibility,
And immaturity,
But, hey, it's not my fault!

I may look like an adult,
But I'm really
Just a kid!

AUTHOR'S COMMENTS

It is not unusual for many of us to cling to immaturity. It's like the "Peter Pan Syndrome." You reason that the grown-up world has too many demands and unrealistic expectations. It's too risky to grow up.

If your childhood had no fun in it, you may be clinging to it, waiting for things to change. It's not unreasonable to imagine someone will come along to take care of you and make sure all your needs are met, like they should have been when you were a child.

This rescuing person can be the responsible one, and at last you can now play. You can get stuck at the emotional level where trauma has occurred. Your body grows older, but you remain emotionally immature.

THOUGHTS TO JOURNAL

• Do I see myself as immature in some areas?

• Have I fully accepted responsibility for myself?

• Do I fantasize that I will be rescued in some way – financially, relationally, professionally?

PRAYER

Dear Lord,

Please show me where parts of me may have become stuck, and perhaps I made a vow never to be a grown-up. Grant me wisdom and support to continue the challenging journey of maturity, self responsibility, and eventual responsibility for others as well. I choose to grow into all that you have planned for me and trust you to be the one who provides for and takes care of me.

LET'S PRETEND

Let's pretend!
Let's pretend it doesn't hurt
When Mommy's sick
And doesn't have energy,
And doesn't seem to care.

Let's pretend it doesn't hurt
That I can't make her happy
No matter how good I am.

There's no time for me.
No attention either,
But "Don't worry, Mommy,"
I'm pretending it doesn't hurt.

Years later I forget I pretended
It doesn't hurt.
I guard the pain with
Carefully constructed arsenal.

"Others had it worse,"
"I should be grateful for what I had,"
"It's not a big deal."

I can't talk about it.
I'm loyal to my family.
It's like betraying the very person
I spent a childhood trying to keep happy.

Besides, if I allowed myself to see
What really happened to me,
I'd have to remember to stop pretending
And really remember

And feel -
The very pain I've spent a lifetime pretending
Didn't hurt.

PRETENDING DOESN'T FIX IT

Pretending doesn't fix it,
My child.

It seems like pretending helps
Because the pain doesn't reach you anymore.

But you had to separate yourself
From truth
And the price was high.

You chose not to feel
And couldn't go back
To being real.

You chose to believe lies,
Make up excuses,
Blame yourself -

Anything -
To not have
To know the truth
And feel the pain it brings.

But truth is your friend.
It causes you to walk in the light.
It brings the pieces of the puzzle together.

It's not about blame.
It's not about denial.
It's about being healed,
Becoming whole,

Knitting back
The dropped and fragmented parts
That pretended
Your reality wasn't true.

Receive the truth!
Trust the Healer!
Walk in the light!
Be made whole!

STAY AND FEEL

Stay! Stay! Stay!
Don't run away!

Feel! Feel! Feel!
The pain is real!

Touch the wound.
Stop pretending
It doesn't hurt.

It's safe now
To stop denying.

You won't be engulfed
Overwhelmed, destroyed.

But you'll feel...
And be sad, and angry
And hurt.

It's all there
Waiting to be felt.

Visit the wounded place.
Stay long enough to
Experience

All that you couldn't manage
As a child.

You're grown up now.
Bring the grown up part to the past
And show compassion
To the helpless, needy, abandoned child.

The child is waiting for you to come,
To stay,
To feel and cry together
Before you bring that little one
Into yourself.
Home.

It makes all the difference!

AUTHOR'S COMMENTS

It is so easy for us to move into denial as a defense against pain. Denial is a God-given help when you encounter early trauma, beyond your ability as a child to handle.

This denial is meant to be temporary, until the day you can allow yourself to know what you experienced and process it with the knowledge of a more mature you. Often the skill of a counselor will help in your healing.

You must show emotional care and empathy to this younger part of you, understanding the pain he or she had to endure. Let the child-part cry, and you, as the grown part, can grieve together. Invite that younger part into your heart and let that part know you are loving and welcoming him or her into yourself.

THOUGHTS TO JOURNAL

• Have I ever thought of talking to a younger part of me?

• How do I feel toward that younger part?

• Am I angry or ashamed or want to stay disconnected?

• Can I listen to how this part of me feels?

PRAYER

Dear Lord,

Please show me where parts of my past are waiting for me to acknowledge and love them. Help me step into truth about my history and stop pretending. Help me to admit how I really felt and grieve my losses. Thank you that you are my Comforter and Healer.

I DON'T KNOW

I don't know.
It's so hard to decide.

This is difficult.
What if I make the wrong choice?

I hear your opinion.
I know your desires.
I want to please you.

I don't know what I want.
I have no opinion.
It's safer that way.

If I can do what you want
Then you'll be happy
And I'll be OK.

No argument. No conflict.
Everyone happy.
"How can I help."
"Here I am."
"Use me."

Let me be sacrificed
On the altar of your needs.
You are more important than I.

It doesn't matter anyway.
I don't know what I want.
I've never had a say.

YOU CAN KNOW

You can know,
You can choose,
You can decide, my child.

I designed you to
Think and feel and create
And know what you know.

I delight in your discoveries
Of life and relationships and self.

Your opinions and thoughts
Are important to me.
I am concerned about the things
That concern you.

Others are not more important than you.
You were not created to worship them
Over Me.

Your power to keep others happy
Is limited.
Don't put your happiness in their care.

Your value and worth is not in their opinion.
Your value and worth is in my opinion,
And I call you Beloved!

You are safe in my arms
With all your feelings, questions and thoughts.
I will guide you into all truth
As you let me.

You won't always do it right
But you can learn.

You can decide and you can know.
Keep trusting and learning
And you will grow.

LEAVING YOU BEHIND

I've spent a lifetime
Leaving my younger self behind.

You're an embarrassment to me,
Just like you seemed to be
To everyone else.

Now I assault you with the same words
You hoped someday to escape.

"You're stupid."
"You should know better."
"Why can't you get it right?"

I put you with people
Who hurt you now
Like you were hurt before.

I set you up in situations
Of familiar pain.

Then I get angry at you
For hurting,
For being angry,
Because nothing's changed.

Get away from me!
I don't want you to exist!

I'm your own worst enemy.
I'm yourself.

LEFT BEHIND

I am small.
I am weak.
I am sad.

I know I embarrass you.
I always mess up.

I can't help myself.
I don't know how.

I will be quiet now.
I'll disappear.

I'll wait
Like a caterpillar
In a cocoon.

I don't know about butterflies.
I don't feel
Anything
Anymore.

When I am shutdown,
Lifeless,
Still,
You are affected.

But you don't know that
And I can't tell you
For I am helpless.

You are my hope for freedom
But you've left me behind.

ALONE

I don't know how it happened.
I didn't want it so.

I thought I would always be together,
Just like at the beginning.

I never knew life apart from me.
In me I lived and breathed.

But somehow I got separated from the me I knew.
It was so very painful.

I depended upon that me for everything.
Did I make her go away?

Please don't leave me alone like this.
I am frightened!

Where are you?
I am lonely!

I NEED YOU!

I run frantically
Looking for help.

Tugging on coat sleeves
"Will you listen to me?"

Knocking on doors
"Will you take care of me?"

Everything is so big
And I'm so small!

I don't know how to do it.
I won't survive at all!

I'm alone

All alone

So alone

PLEASE HELP ME!

TOGETHER

Someone is looking for you.
He hears your cry,
He knows your need.
He's here right now,
He's been here all along.

Don't shy back.
He won't hurt you.
Jesus loves the little children.

Take His hand.
He's leading you to a new place.
There's a grown-up part of you now
Who can help.

She can be there for you
If you let her.

She can learn your needs,
Listen to your pain,
Hold you in her arms,
Find ways to heal your wounds
If you choose.

She brings you to me,
For in me she lives and breathes
And has her being.

You are part of her.
You need never be alone.
Wherever she is, you will be.
Wherever I am, she will be.

Your grown-up self and I are together now,
Never to be separated.

I will meet her needs
And she will meet yours.

She will be the nurturer you never knew.
I will be the source of her love and care.

Depend on her as she depends on me.
You've been found now,
From your loneliness you're free.

AUTHOR'S COMMENTS

God has created a built-in defense system in children where part of their emotional self can split off from itself when faced with an overwhelming situation. Little children have the ability to dissociate from their abuse so they can continue to function in everyday life.

Is it possible you have left parts of yourself behind, in the past, in memories that may have split off? It's nothing to be ashamed of. A child's ability to split helps keep them sane.

Denial helps you not to feel overwhelmed when you have no ability to process the conflicting emotions. As an adult the protectiveness of denial is now a hindrance to true freedom. Give yourself permission to explore your past. There is great healing in coming into truth and wholeness within yourself.

THOUGHTS TO JOURNAL

• What is my earliest memory?

• If you have no recall before age seven,
you may have some lost parts within yourself.

• Are there memories I have of myself that
I am angry or embarrassed about?

• Am I willing to reach out in kindness to that part?

PRAYER

Dear Lord,

Help me to know the truth about myself. Let me show love and kindness to any wounded child part inside of me who is feeling rejection. Thank you, Jesus, that you have searched for me and found me, like the little lost lamb. Thank you that you have accepted and never rejected me. Help me do the same for myself.

TAUGHT TO HATE MYSELF

You taught me to hate
Myself, Mom.

In a thousand little ways
You made innuendos
That I was no good.

I got the message -
That I wasn't really wanted,
That I was an inconvenience,
That I interrupted your life.

You taught me well.

And now I no longer
Have to hear you
Put me down.

I find thousands of little ways
To agree with your teachings.

I've taken up
Where you left off.

Your thoughts and words have fused
With mine.

And I contain
The message:

"That I'm not wanted,
Not worthy of love and goodness
From myself or others."

You can be proud of me, Mom,
For now I hate myself
Just like you taught me.

SUBSTITUTE

I wasn't looking for it.
It just came along.

It saw the gaping hole in my heart,
The unmet longings,
The lonely despair, the isolation and pain.

"I can fix that," it boasted.
"I can do it quick."
"I can do it every time you
Invite me in."

I pondered.
People had hurt me, used me, left me.
Maybe there was something here
In this new thing.

Others had tried it before.
I could do it like them.

What the hell, why not?

I invited it in,
And it was wonderful!
There was no more pain or sorrow...

Swirling in delight
I felt so strong and powerful.

I knew I had the answer.
I didn't need people,
I just needed it.

Often we spent time together.
It always delivered
Just like it promised.

There was a price to pay,
But I ignored it.

The concern it caused could be easily handled
By one more use,

And then another,
And yet another,
And, my dear God,
Another,
And another,
and another.

Who was using who?

I am trapped, I am sinking, I am gone.
There is only pain and sorrow.

HELP ME LORD

Help me Lord!

I have sinned!
I am trapped in despair!

I am powerless
Over this thing
That holds me captive.

I invited it in
And it has taken me over.

It promised me happiness,
A way out of pain,
A fuller life.

It lied!
I have been deceived!
I am dying!

I think I want out
But it's become part of me.

Can I live without it?
Will I stay alive with it?

I'm scared, real scared!

Who am I anyway?
Maybe I'm more it than me.

I'm at the bottom, Lord.
Can you find me?
Can you help me?

PLEASE
PLEASE

HELP!

I WILL HELP

I will help,
Calls Jesus, the Good Shepherd.
I hear your cry!

I delight to rescue you
From the hand
Of the enemy.

I defeated him on Calvary.
The power of sin over you
Is broken.

Let me lift you from the pit.
Trust my strong arms under you.

You looked in the wrong place
To heal your pain.
I am your Source
Of healing and life.

You tried to meet your needs
With substitutes.

Only I can satisfy you.
Find your passion in me

My way is pure and right and good.
In me you will find life
And that abundantly.

I am your Strength in weakness.
Do not be afraid.
I am with you and will never leave you.

In me you will overcome.
My Spirit within you is strong.

You are my beloved child.
Sin no longer has a part in you.

You can walk in victory.
Defeat temptation by
Greater passion.

Worship and love me with all your heart.
My light always overcomes the darkness.

I am here to deliver,
Redeem, restore,
Protect, empower
And love you with all my heart!

A GREATER PASSION

My heart was made for you, Lord.
No one else can fill your place.

You alone of all creation
Give life meaning by your grace.

Substitutes have come and gone
They've left their pain and sorrow.

No one else can satisfy.
Only you redeem tomorrow.

You do not use us,
Hurt, abuse us.
Your love is pure and free.

You love us
Heal us, keep us
For all eternity.

Thank you, thank you, Jesus!
You are awesome in your grace.

Thank you, thank you, Jesus!
I only seek your face.

May my passion be toward you, Lord,
Not toward things that pull me down.

I want to honor you, Lord.
Be my glory and my crown!

AUTHORS COMMENTS

Underneath all addictions is a broken place in one's soul. If you had abuse in childhood, you may have tried to fill the unhealed pain with a substance, person, or thing.

The original pain can be temporarily quieted by your "drug of choice," but as you may have discovered, your attempt to heal your heart and quiet the torment has only created more turmoil and pain.

Now you crave the very thing that is destroying you. Admitting you are helpless and crying out to God for rescue is humbling, but powerful.

A recovering addict can become a brand new person who is sober, honest, humble, grateful and loving.

THOUGHTS TO JOURNAL

• Have I tried to bury my pain under substances, people, or things?

• What are my reasons for wanting to escape?

• How far back does the pain go?

• Am I willing to talk to someone?

PRAYER

Dear Lord,

I repent before you that I have tried to manage my life apart from you. Lord, I have failed and feel such shame. Please have mercy on me and deliver me from my ungodly cravings. Help me face the woundedness that I have been stuffing down and denying. Take me to the source of pain and help me forgive and release everyone who has harmed me. Come into my heart and life, Lord Jesus, and save me from my sins. Be my Savior and Deliverer. Thank you, Jesus.

About The Author

Trudy Colflesh has had a tender heart and sensitive spirit since childhood. She grew up in the home of a Presbyterian minister and saw her parents seek to meet others' needs in Christian love and service.

Trudy became active in service herself in high school and college. She graduated from the College of Wooster, Ohio, married her college sweetheart and worked several years in a Presbyterian church as a Director of Christian Education.

For many years, Trudy was a stay-at-home mom and active in volunteer church service. She and her husband, George, have two natural children, Christopher and Karen, a son Michael, adopted when he was ten years old, and have fostered two young boys.

When Karen was almost seven, she became ill with leukemia and despite doing all possible to save her, she died within seven months. Out of this painful time, Trudy wrote the book *Too Precious To Die* and traveled around the country speaking at Women's Aglow Fellowships and appearing on CBN and other TV and radio programs.

Having opportunity to minister to hurting people, as she herself was healing, Trudy felt the Lord calling her to go into the field of counseling. She went to graduate school and earned her Master's degree in Counseling at Montclair State University, New Jersey, in 1990 and became a Licensed Professional Counselor.

Since that time, Trudy has worked as a Christian Counselor, ministering hope and healing to countless clients. She has listened to her own soul cry and pursued recovery, as well as listened to the hearts of her clients. She knows with certainty, that out of the painful issues of life, comes a sure belief that Jesus Christ knows our emotional pain, hears our soul cry and brings us His Presence to comfort and heal.

"And we know that in all things God works for the good of those who love him, who have been called according to his purpose." (Romans 8:28)

Trudy is available for telephone counseling and coaching. If you would like to set up an appointment, please contact her at: Trudy@Encouraginghope.com. Comments or questions may also be addressed to Trudy at this location.

SEE OTHER BOOKS IN THE SoulCry Series

Book 2
Abandonment, Emotional Wounding, Relationships, Fear, Sadness, Rejection

Book 3
Enmeshment, Identity, Pain, Inadequacy, Shame, Dependency, Dissociation

Book 4
Sexual Abuse, Denial, SRA, Dissociation, Betrayal, Control, Identity, Trauma

Book 5
Dissociation, Suffering, SRA, Sexual Abuse, Forgiveness, Comfort, Healing, Joy

Book 6
Shame, Failure, Perfection, SRA, Dissociation, Anger, Sexual Intimacy, Truth, Acceptance

Book 7
Worth, Denial, Dissociation, Ritual Abuse, Rejection, Sexual Abuse, Surrender, Love, Healing

Book 8
Enmeshment, Attachment, Self Worth, Suffering, Occult Bondage, Generational Iniquities, Mercy, Freedom, Integration

Book 9
Denial, Guilt, Shame, Lost Identity, Lost Time, Reputation, Dissociation, Programming, Comfort, Safety, Original Self

All books are available to order at:

www.encouraginghope.com/books
www.amazon.com/author/trudycolflesh

Too Precious To Die

Seven year old Karen Colflesh was diagnosed with AML, Acute Myelomonocytic Leukemia, a rare form of the disease not usually found in children.

Too Precious To Die, is an intimate, personal account of Karen's battle against this deadly disease. It is as triumphant as it is tragic. Karen's courageous fight was an inspiration to all who came in contact with her.

This story shows the victories the Lord God won on Karen's behalf, and the healing miracles He demonstrated throughout her illness.

However, despite all the doctor's skill and the faith of many, Karen was called home to Heaven in a glorious vision.
Trudy shares how she and the family overcame their grief and found answers and comfort to Karen's early death.

Trudy has shared Karen's story throughout the country, speaking at Women's Aglow meetings, as well as on radio and TV.
She and her husband George were guests of Pat Robinson on the 700 Club.

This is a moving, compelling story that draws the reader into the experience.

www.ingramcontent.com/pod-product-compliance
Lightning Source LLC
LaVergne TN
LVHW021538080426
835509LV00019B/2709